Original title:
The Weirdness of Life, Wrapped in a Poem

Copyright © 2025 Creative Arts Management OÜ
All rights reserved.

Author: Samuel Kensington
ISBN HARDBACK: 978-1-80566-179-5
ISBN PAPERBACK: 978-1-80566-474-1

Enchanted Misfits

Gnomes play chess with squirrels,
While birds trade tales of dreams.
A cat in boots does twirl,
And prances through the beams.

Cakes float through the air,
With frosting filled with cheer.
A frog sings in despair,
To a crowd that cannot hear.

Playful Reflections

Mirrors laugh at my face,
While shadows dance around.
A dog can keep the pace,
Yet he's nowhere to be found.

Bubbles whisper secrets,
To the clouds high above.
A snail chases regrets,
In a world full of love.

Chimeras of the Everyday

Flying fish in the park,
While hedgehogs wear their hats.
A toaster sings 'til dark,
With a wink and chatty spats.

Rainbows sparkle on trees,
As worms put on a show.
Where the sun tickles bees,
And grasshoppers steal the glow.

Fluctuations of the Mind

Thoughts dance like loose balloons,
In a sky of endless blue.
Where time plays silly tunes,
And the clock wears funny shoes.

Dreams tumble down the stairs,
In a race with sleepy heads.
Offering playful dares,
To the night before it spreads.

Strangeness Lurking Beneath

Beneath the surface, oddities reside,
Where llamas wear hats, and fish take pride.
The sun may just wink, a squirrel might dance,
Inviting us all to join in the prance.

Socks may wander, shoes stay near,
Finding treasures that spark laughter and cheer.
With each step we take on this wobbly ground,
Strangeness lurks, and joy can be found.

Unexpected Harmonies of Existence

A cat plays piano, a dog sings along,
Balloons float by with a very nice song.
Toasters may chatter, while crumpets send texts,
Delighting our minds with humor and hexes.

Clouds gather round for a comedy show,
As ducks take the stage in a line-up to blow.
Giggles reside where the oddities play,
In mismatched shoes, we all dance away.

Kaleidoscope of Curious Encounters

Marbles rolled out of a candy store flat,
A rabbit in glasses reads quietly—chat!
Unexpected twists, a giraffe with a tie,
Each moment unfolds, and we wonder why.

Watch buttercups gossip with curious bees,
While moonlit llamas serve up warm teas.
In this spinning wheel, colors combine,
Curiosity blooms, and laughter aligns.

A Symphony of Misfit Thoughts

A violin made from a shoe on the floor,
Whistles and giggles collide with a roar.
Odd melodies ripple in whimsical air,
Where thoughts dance around without a single care.

Mismatched socks begin to hum tunes,
As pancakes juggle beneath colorful moons.
This symphony plays to the odd and the out,
Embracing the chaos with joyous shout.

Melodies of the Absurd

A cat walks by in a top hat,
With shoes too big for its feet.
It dances along the sidewalk,
Like it's got some secret beat.

A toaster talks to a spoon,
While the clock just ticks and grins.
They plan a party for the moon,
To celebrate their whims.

A tree throws a leaf confetti,
As squirrels juggle nuts and pies.
Balloons float up, all too petty,
Whispering their little lies.

And so we laugh at all these quirks,
In a world that prances wide.
Finding joy in silly works,
As absurdities collide.

Unlikely Harmonies

A fish in shoes sings a tune,
As a dog plays the saxophone.
Together they rock the afternoon,
While riding a giant ice cream cone.

A llama stars on a game show,
With questions about spaghetti and rain.
The audience laughs with a big 'whoa!',
As the poor host goes completely insane.

A cactus dons a feathered mask,
In a ballet with bright jellybeans.
They dance and twirl, what a task!
The audience stomps, as it leans.

In the end, all's a revelry,
Finding joy where none should be.
These tunes of oddity set us free,
With giggles in a jubilee.

Parables of Peculiarity

A hedgehog writes in fine calligraphy,
With ink made from a rainbow's hue.
It tells tales of catfish in trivia,
Who argue about skies of blue.

A penguin wearing sunglasses struts,
While the popcorn machine now sings.
It spills kernels and giggles in ruts,
Creating a dance as it flings.

An octopus juggles with glee,
Juggling donuts instead of balls.
Each toss and catch, what a sight to see,
As laughter echoes from the walls.

In peculiar twists, we find our cheer,
In moments that break the mold.
For in the oddity, we all endear,
And let the stories unfold.

Subtle Surrealism

A teacup floats upon a breeze,
While a goldfish wears a crown.
They sip nectar from the trees,
As lilacs bop up and down.

A squirrel rides a bicycle,
On a road made of candy leaves.
He whistles tunes quite cyclical,
While the sun giggles and weaves.

Mushrooms wear tiny raincoats,
As a raincloud drops its glee.
Their dance is like playful anecdotes,
In a realm of oddity.

In this chaos, we find our gaze,
At the wonders twisting wide.
For even in the strangest phase,
The heart finds joy inside.

Doodles on the Canvas of Time

In the clock's tick-tock dance, strange shadows play,
An egg in a hat says it's a sunny day.
Cats wear sunglasses, lounging on the roof,
While fish in the pond are constructing a booth.

A chicken with glasses reads a tall book,
As ants in tuxedos practice their look.
Rain falls in jellybeans, sweet on the ground,
And cows do the cha-cha, all around town.

The moon sings a lullaby, slightly off-key,
To stars doing cartwheels, wild and so free.
A worm on a skateboard rolls past with a grin,
While flowers decide it's a good time to spin.

Giggles erupt from trees dressed in plaid,
Tickling the branches, chasing the sad.
Each moment's a riddle, a puzzle to crack,
As life doodles sweetly, no turning back.

Unexpected Flights of Fancy

A squirrel in a tux begins his grand flight,
With balloons tied to paws, he ascends through the night.
A pizza in hand waves goodbye from the ground,
As unicorns giggle, they whirl all around.

Exploding confetti from tall, frosty cakes,
Each slice tells a story that wiggles and quakes.
Ducks tap dance on puddles, all wearing big shoes,
While spaghetti noodles play hopscotch with blues.

A rainbow retreats with a wink and a hop,
While jellybeans roll, never wanting to stop.
The sun wears a top hat and spins like a fawn,
As creatures of whimsy just laugh 'til the dawn.

In alleyways vibrant with colors so bold,
Time drapes its fabrics in glittering gold.
Riding the breezes, surprises unfold,
As life dances wildly, its stories retold.

Unspoken Anomalies

Cats in bowties might rule the night,
Sunsets whisper secrets out of sight.
Fish ride bicycles, quite the delight,
While squirrels debate if cheese is right.

Birds in tuxedos hold court on a branch,
Balloons float by in a lively dance.
Umbrellas open for a sunny chance,
Life spins in circles, like a wild prance.

Dancing with the Bizarre

Pickles hold hands with jellybeans too,
In a waltz of wonders, oh what a view!
Dancing shoes tap on clouds made of dew,
While socks conspire to form a new crew.

Worms play the banjo as night falls in place,
While butterflies giggle and join the race.
The moon wears a hat, it's quite out of space,
And stars join the chorus, full of ace.

Laughter Beneath the Surface

In the fridge, a pickle tells a good joke,
Mice plan a heist without making a poke.
Toasters dream deep, they're never a smoke,
While the bread laughs hard, what a quirky cloak!

Ants wear sunglasses, their anthem is grand,
Creating a band in a crumb-laden land.
Tarzan the snail swings a tiny hand,
As chaos brews up in this whimsical band.

Unraveled Paradoxes

A clock that ticks, but never goes slow,
Tells tales of time in its rhythmic flow.
Yet it pauses sometimes, just to bestow,
Confusion in moments, oh what a show!

A penguin in Hawaii prefers sun on sand,
While elephants sprint in a waltzing band.
Mirrors reflect dreams that stretch out of hand,
And laughter erupts where the oddities stand.

Fluctuations of the Unseen

Invisible things just dance around,
Like socks that go missing, never found.
A cat that speaks in riddles so bright,
As it stares at the wall, lost in its flight.

A toaster that sings with a voice so grand,
While bread jumps aboard, it just can't stand.
The fridge hums softly, a lullaby tune,
Makes midnight snacks feel like a grand festoon.

The clock spins backward like a thrill ride,
Each tick and tock is a witty guide.
Life's quirks unfold, with flair and cheer,
In this circus of time, where oddities steer.

Oddities in the Garden of Days

In the garden of days, where time grows weird,
There blooms a flower that's laughed at and sneered.
It whispers secrets of rain and sun,
And dances lightly as if it's just begun.

A snail in a bowtie moves with such grace,
While the ants throw a party, all over the place.
The trees wear hats, and the wind gives a wink,
All nature conspires, or so it might think.

With daisies sipping tea and the grass playing chess,
Each moment's a romp, never less, never less.
In this odd little realm where laughter prevails,
Every day's stories are crafted like tales.

Tangents and Twists of Fate's Design

Life's a twisty road, with signs misaligned,
Where the coffee pot grumbles, and 'time' redefined.
Cats wear bowties, and dogs sport a cap,
As turtles discuss life over a silent nap.

Each corner we turn, there's a prancing hare,
Reciting old poems with style and flair.
The clouds wear pajamas, as stars join the fun,
While planets play tag, in a big cosmic run.

The universe chuckles, a jester's delight,
As each little mishap becomes quite a sight.
Fate's design is quirky, a wild paper plane,
With laughter and chaos, it dances in rain.

The Chronicles of Uncommon Journeys

Gather round, friends, for tales untold,
Of journeys so odd, they sparkle like gold.
The bus drives backward, with a wink from the driver,
And a frog in a suit, becoming a high-fiver.

Through forests of lollipops, rivers of cream,
Where unicorns play charades and it's all just a dream.
The path winds through giggles and echoes of glee,
As the air fills with bubbles floating carefree.

With dragons in cafes sipping tea with a miss,
Every moment's a joy, a whimsical bliss.
So grab your odd shoes, let's step out of line,
For the chronicles we write will always shine fine.

Ephemeral Wonders

Balloons are flying, but where do they go?
A sock on the floor, with no friend in tow.
Cats chase their tails like a dance on the ground,
While pancakes land softly, they spin all around.

A sneeze brings confetti from nowhere, oh dear!
Noses turn red in the chill of the cheer.
Dancing in circles, the dogs steal the show,
As jellybeans tangle in pockets of woe.

A snail made of chocolate, so slow, such a treat,
Winks at a cupcake with frosting so sweet.
Clouds shape a dragon, or maybe a shoe,
Each moment unfurls like a dream coming true.

Seagulls debate if they'll dive for a fry,
While shadows play tag in the bright blue sky.
Lollipops whisper secrets to trees,
Every single giggle lifts hearts like a breeze.

The Joy in the Quirky

In the land where the socks make a runaway plan,
Lives a penguin that dances whilst cooking for man.
He juggles with marshmallows, so fluffy and white,
And giggles at goldfish that take off in flight.

A ladybug tap dances on a leaf with flair,
While owls don the latest in feathered wear.
The moon wears sunglasses to block out the sun,
As parrots play poker, just having some fun.

Pineapples gossip about their cool hats,
While giraffes sip lemonade, chatting with bats.
The sunflowers wave at the bees flying by,
And crickets sing praises to the starry sky.

Chickens take selfies while perched on a fence,
Creating a ruckus, oh such common sense.
Burritos wear blankets and snuggle at night,
In a world full of odd, everything feels right.

Fantasies of the Ordinary

A toaster dreams of flying on wings made of bread,
While waffles plot trips to the top of your head.
Pillows hold parties until morning's first light,
Where dreams wear pajamas and dance through the night.

A cup of warm cocoa conspires with tea,
To launch a surprise on sweet candy spree.
A fridge tells the stories of leftovers stored,
While dust bunnies battle for crumbs they've adored.

Spoons take the stage in a musical play,
While forks strum the strings of a macaroon ballet.
A clock cracks a joke, and the tick-tock replies,
In the kitchen, the madness brings laughter and sighs.

Noses get twitchy from tickling dust,
As chairs have a chat about comfort and trust.
The curtain of chaos in cushions that sway,
Around every corner, life's quirky ballet.

Echoes of the Unusual

In a land where the teacups grow legs and can dance,
Daisies wear spectacles, holding intellect's chance.
The butter floats gently like clouds in the air,
While spoons glide on ice, pulling pizzas to share.

A llama that raps with a flair so delightful,
Cracks jokes with the clocks, oh, it's so insightful.
Frogs sing the blues to the stars shining bright,
As fish throw a party in the pale moonlight.

The sky likes to giggle with rain purely free,
While clouds dress in colors of jelly and tea.
Candles sing softly, their wax melting slow,
In this world that spins on the whim of a show.

A bicycle jaunts through a puddle of laughs,
While penquins play chess in their smart woolen scarves.
Echoes of oddness ring true in each turn,
In the curious chaos, we all start to learn.

Tapestry of the Strange

In the sky, fish dance and sing,
While the dogs wear hats, oh what a fling!
Cats in goggles chase the breeze,
Teacups argue under the trees.

Mirrors reflect a world askew,
With Django cats and a wizard or two.
Elephants prance on tiny feet,
As clouds rain jellybeans, what a treat!

The flowers gossip without a care,
And the moon plays hopscotch in midair.
Kites and pinwheels laugh and glide,
In this odd circus, we all abide.

Laughter echoes in the twilight hue,
As squirrels debate on a high hill's view.
Life spins a tale of the absurd,
In this tapestry, joy is stirred.

Echoing Anomalies

Jack in the box with a talking spoon,
Dances with shadows under the moon.
A picnic on clouds with rainbow bread,
Where flamingos plan their dance ahead.

Phones that sing and socks that joke,
As mushrooms play chess in the oak.
Chickens chatting on a slide,
While umbrellas float on the silly ride.

Stars whistling tunes in the cosmic night,
As high-fiving owls take flight.
Blenders grinding out sweet dreams,
In this wild place, everything gleams.

With every step, a new surprise,
Where laughter bubbles and joy flies.
In a world where oddities blend,
Life's echo whispers, it's just pretend.

Shimmering Irregularities

Balloons that giggle, jellyfish sway,
As pickles drive cars on a sunny day.
The rainbows shout with a vivid cheer,
And magic beans bloom every year.

Radishes dance in polka dot hats,
While frogs wear boots and chat with rats.
Juggling kittens spin in delight,
As candy canes glisten, oh what a sight!

Teapots whistle the tunes of a bard,
With goldfish making life not too hard.
Daisies paint their petals bright,
In this strange land, all feels right.

Giggles bubble from every nook,
As the world unfolds like a lively book.
In shimmering tones of the uncanny,
Life's a quirky, delightful fanny!

Jigsaw of the Unconventional

A puzzle with pieces that jump and run,
While tigers skateboard just for fun.
The clock strikes two with a splash of paint,
And lollipops tell stories without restraint.

Frogs in bow ties give fashion advice,
While spoons debate the strength of rice.
Marshmallows run in a silly trot,
As fizzy fizz drinks turn thoughts to knot!

Parrots reciting ancient lore,
With clouds playing chess on the kitchen floor.
Life's puzzles fit an odd old twist,
Where cats make muffins, surely a mist!

In a jigsaw of giggles and glee,
As cupcakes fly up from the sea.
The unconventional thrives, oh so grand,
In this vibrant, zany, wondrous land.

Surreal Hues of Everyday Moments

A cat in a hat, sipping tea,
While ducks dance in shoes, can't you see?
The clock hands are stuck, twelve past the sun,
And who knew that socks could actually run?

A fish on a bike rides past the park,
Chasing a squirrel who's lighting a spark.
Lollipops grow on the old oak trees,
And ants hold a meeting, discussing the breeze.

Serenade of the Unexplained

A toaster sings songs of buttery toast,
While shadows do cartwheels, a ghost does a coast.
Fish in bow ties gossip with birds in a suit,
As the moon pulls a prank, and the stars shoot the loot.

A turtle with glasses reads poetry loud,
While rain clouds applaud, forming a crowd.
Indeed, logic has packed, gone out for a stroll,
And reality just signed up for a role!

Quirky Tapestry of Time

Umbrellas grow roots in the soft velvet air,
And jellybeans dance with a flamboyant flair.
The skies melt like ice cream, delightful and sweet,
While the grass giggles softly beneath my feet.

A raccoon in slippers steals cookies at night,
Charming the fridge with his band of delight.
With spoons all a-tango and forks in ballet,
Every odd corner steals boredom away!

The Anomaly Parade

Parrots in suits march down the lane,
With cupcakes for hats, they chant in refrain.
Yo-yos are flying, while balloons take a bow,
And rain coats applaud from the edge of a cow.

Sandwiches giggle, all dressed in their best,
As the sun winks at clouds, in a curious jest.
Reality wiggles, in an unlikely charade,
Join in the fun, there's no need to evade!

Eccentric Reflections in a Starlit Pond

A squirrel in a tuxedo, sipping tea,
Dancing with the shadows of a nearby tree.
The moon wearing glasses, lending a hand,
As frogs play chess on the soft, wet land.

Fish in bow ties swim by with flair,
Kicking up bubbles that float in the air.
A raccoon recites lines from Shakespeare's best,
While crickets cheer on, all dressed in their zest.

Lily pads giggle as they float all around,
Wishing on shooting stars that barely touch ground.
Every ripple tells secrets too silly to keep,
In this splashing pond where the quirks never sleep.

The Poetry of Peculiarities

A cat who thinks it's a leading man,
Practicing lines in a search for a plan.
Dogs roll their eyes, but they can't resist,
Joining the chaos in this weird twist.

Balloons that converse, telling tales so grand,
Of drifting on breezes in a faraway land.
A lizard in shades, sunbathing with pride,
While ants march in tune as a curious guide.

The paint on the fence is a Picasso delight,
Spraying odd shapes in the late, dead of night.
Each brushstroke a giggle, a chuckle, a cheer,
In every odd corner, there's laughter to hear.

Paradoxical Dreams in Dappled Light

A toaster that toasts with a wink and a grin,
Spinning strange tales of the bread tucked within.
While curtains discuss which way they should sway,
As sunlight prances, inviting a play.

A clock with two hands that dance in a race,
Losing their grip on the concept of space.
When shadows grow tall, they begin to debate,
About which is better—a tall tale or fate?

The floorboards laugh softly at each little step,
Puppets on strings, all with purpose and pep.
In dappled light's glow, each moment declared,
Is filled with odd wonders that nobody dared.

Anomalies in the Fabric of Day

A bicycle floats on a river of cream,
Pedaled by seagulls that wiggle and beam.
Chickens in bowler hats dance in a line,
Clucking to rhythms, oh so divine!

The sun waves goodbye to the moon in disguise,
Trading mismatched socks as they spin through the skies.
Clouds wear top hats, floating high on a whim,
While laughter erupts as the light starts to dim.

Grass chews on sunlight, savoring beams,
As wishes take flight like fantastical dreams.
In this day of oddities, cheer fills the air,
As quirks mingle freely, showing just how much they care.

The Unexpected Laughter of Chance

A squirrel stole my sandwich,
Then danced like a star.
I laughed so hard, I stumbled,
And fell near the car.

Life throws us odd moments,
Like socks lost in the wash.
Uncles who sing off-key,
And cats that like to nosh.

A bike with a flat tire,
Turns into a wild ride.
We roll down the hill softly,
With laughter as our guide.

In this circus of nonsense,
We're juggling dreams and frowns.
But in the midst of chaos,
Are clowns who wear big crowns.

A Journey Through the Bizarre

A monkey stole my flip-flop,
Then gave a cheeky grin.
I chased him through the garden,
With echoes of my kin.

Bananas have their secrets,
They giggle on the vine.
Every fruit has a story,
That bends the line of time.

The postman talks to shadows,
And argues with the moon.
His letters fly like pigeons,
They'll land here very soon.

In this strange carnival,
Where oddities collide.
We'll dance with the absurd,
And take it all in stride.

Poems from the Other Side of Ordinary

Balloons whisper sweet secrets,
As they float out to sea.
Fish wear tiny top hats,
And swim so gracefully.

Dancing forks in the kitchen,
Make spaghetti with flair.
While a toaster serenades,
The bread with utmost care.

The cat guards our secrets,
With a wise, ancient gaze.
Finding socks under sofas,
In her peculiar ways.

Each moment's a treasure,
Wrapped in giggles and cheer.
Embracing the strange stories,
That keep our hearts sincere.

Eccentric Wanderings in the Human Heart

A pickle jar philosopher,
Spouts wisdom with a grin.
He claims that life's a dance,
With pickles dipped in sin.

A book reads itself loudly,
With all its pages torn.
While paperclips converse,
About how they were born.

In a world made of jelly,
And cereal that's gold,
We ride on marshmallow clouds,
With stories yet untold.

Let's toss our mundanities,
Into the hazy sky.
For in the strange and funny,
Is where our smiles lie.

Celebrating the Unconventional

In a world where ducks wear hats,
And cats recite Shakespeare on mats.
We dance with squirrels, so spry and quick,
Painting our dreams with a splash of pink.

Jellybeans rain on Wednesday nights,
While the toaster jingles and invites.
Our neighbors juggle with broken lights,
As we laugh until the morning delights.

Socks mismatched, but oh so bold,
In colors that shimmer like tales of old.
We toast to the quirks that always thrill,
And take a nap on the windowsill.

A time machine made from a broom,
Takes us to a land where smiles bloom.
With each odd turn, we'd only grin,
For life's best surprises lie just within.

Mirth in Mayhem

Spaghetti grows on the trees outside,
And pickles dance with glee in stride.
Hiccups that rhyme, a comedic feat,
As we prance with joy on jelly feet.

The moon wears glasses, a sight so fine,
While the stars do the limbo, feeling divine.
Our bread sings songs whilst the olives cheer,
Creating a ruckus that's entirely clear.

Pigs fly by in their puffy shorts,
Winking and giggling with cheer of sorts.
With every flap and unsteady route,
Laughter erupts, there's no time for doubt.

So gather 'round for this ridiculous show,
With confetti clouds that bubble and flow.
Embrace the chaos and join the fun,
For mirth in mayhem has only begun!

Serendipitous Twists

A pigeon wearing a purple tie,
Confesses secrets to the sky.
While rainbows taste like lemonade,
Our worries fade, they're so delayed.

A goldfish recites philosophy,
As pineapples giggle with glee.
In a world where socks are held in court,
We jest and play with no retort.

Giraffes in roller skates glide by,
Waving to llamas on beds of pie.
We spin in circles, then tumble down,
As kooky creatures tour the town.

With upside-down clocks and chocolate rain,
We toss away all the mundane pain.
In serendipity's quirky embrace,
Life dances lightly, never a trace.

Laughter in Disguise

A walrus speaks in riddles of cheese,
While ants play chess beneath the trees.
Shoelaces tie themselves in knots,
As we giggle at their silly plots.

A pizza with a grin greets the day,
Winking at pineapples in disarray.
With umbrellas held high in bright paint,
We march through puddles, boisterous and quaint.

Bananas in pajamas spin 'round the floor,
Tickling kittens who cannot ignore.
Whispers of joy fill the morning air,
As we delve into fun without a care.

In a realm where oddballs come alive,
And laughter wears a jester's guise.
Let's cherish the quirky, the odd, the sweet,
For life, my friend, is a whimsical treat.

Unraveling Threads of the Oddly Familiar

In a world where cats wear hats,
And dogs sip tea with grace,
I found a fish on roller skates,
With sparkles on its face.

Balloons float by to greet the sun,
While umbrellas dance in glee,
A pickle sings a merry tune,
As squirrels climb a tree.

Mysteries wrapped in toast and jam,
Pantries filled with dreams,
A fridge that whispers secrets late,
In laughter's silly schemes.

So let's embrace the quirks we find,
With giggles as our guide,
For in the odd, we share our smiles,
And let the joy abide.

When Clocks Spin Backwards

The clock struck four, no wait, it's five,
　　As turtles race the moon,
　　Caffeine dreams in coffee steams,
　　　Awake by afternoon.

Time skips rope and jumps around,
　　As laughter fills the air,
　　A sandwich takes a stroll today,
　　　With socks upon its pair.

Dancing shadows play hide and seek,
　　While robots sip their gin,
　　And every hour's a big surprise,
　　When clocks just spin and spin.

Let's twirl along with time's own twist,
　　With glee from every hour,
　　In this peculiar circus world,
　　We bloom like every flower.

Unconventional Whispers in the Wind

The breeze told tales of fish on bikes,
And clouds that wore bow ties,
As flowers shared their silly jokes,
Underneath the skies.

A rainbow snickers, puddles laugh,
As raindrops tap-dance free,
A smartphone reads the stars at night,
While squirrels sip on tea.

Winds swirl tales of socks misplaced,
In shoes that run away,
With hints of dreams that float like ghosts,
Through every sunny day.

So listen close to nature's quirk,
With smiles that never end,
For in the whispers of the wind,
We find our truest friend.

Confessions of a Curious Mind

I asked a lamp why it glows bright,
It laughed and answered, 'Why not?'
A chair confessed it dreams of flight,
But settles in a spot.

A curious spoon feels quite esteem,
For stirring up some fun,
While mirrors ponder who they are,
When every face is done.

With plants that gossip in the night,
And pillows never sleep,
I scribble down these thoughts galore,
In laughter's joyful leap.

So here I stand, a probe of thoughts,
In laughter's grand parade,
For life's confessions, strange and bright,
Are smiles that never fade.

Dreams in Unfamiliar Colors

Balloons in plaid and polka dots,
Painted skies in pickle pots.
Cats wearing hats and shoes too wide,
Chasing rainbows on a roller slide.

Unicycles ride on tightrope strings,
While fish wear crowns and flapping wings.
Ice cream mountains drip with glee,
As squirrels whistle songs from a tree.

Cactus waltzes with the moonlit night,
And toast starts dancing, oh what a sight!
With each twist and twirl, a chuckle escapes,
As giggles tumble like ginger snaps.

In these dreams where laughter flows,
Life's a circus, everybody knows.
Upside down, fun swirls around,
Where happy thoughts are blissfully found.

Slices of Surrealism

Toast so silly it sings a tune,
With jelly beans hopping around the room.
A clock that melts, as seconds sway,
While elephants skate in a cabaret.

Chairs that giggle, and mirrors wink,
What do they see? Blink and rethink!
Lemonade rivers, sweet, and bright,
Where fish wear shoes and take flight.

Pineapples in suits, they strut their stuff,
Toast to the days that are truly buff.
A lemonade stand that serves with flair,
Sipping sunshine, without a care.

In odd little pies with curious flavors,
The crust celebrates our silly savors.
So slice that surreal and take a bite,
Life's a buffet of pure delight!

Curious Embraces

Hugs from hedgehogs, prickly and sweet,
An orchestra of frogs keeps the beat.
Moonlit penguins dance on the sea,
As stars throw confetti, wild and free.

Pillow fights with clouds, fluffy as can be,
Whispering secrets that tickle the tree.
Marshmallows bounce on spaghetti threads,
While giggling pumpkins hop from their beds.

Bubbles floating filled with laughter,
Chasing echoes—what a disaster!
Each snug embrace from a giggly sprite,
Turns gloomy moments into pure light.

So dance, my dear, on clouds made of dreams,
With curious creatures and magical schemes.
Each hug, a story, a whimsical tale,
Life's most vibrant wind in the sail!

The Dance of the Uncommon

Unicorns prancing in rain-soaked boots,
As dandelions hum and teeny fruits hoot.
Socks mismatched, a fashionable crime,
Dancing on rooftops, oh what a rhyme!

Puppies in bowties sway like pros,
Chasing butterflies that tickle their nose.
Giraffes playing chess, pondering moves,
While kangaroos boogie, in funny grooves.

Balloons chatter while organizing tea,
With tangerines marching, wild and free.
Through laughter and wonder, they whirl about,
Turning the common into a shout!

So twirl in the spotlight, let oddity reign,
In a dance making colors glow bright as grain.
Embrace the kooky, the laughter and cheer,
In this splendid dance, the joy is sincere!

The Poignant Peculiar

In socks of mismatched hue,
I dance with my old shoe.
Chicken crossed the road for fun,
In search of a melting sun.

The toaster sings a funky tune,
While beans hum a subtle croon.
My cat dons a silly hat,
As I ponder: where's the fat?

Odd Serenades of Time

Tick-tock's a playful chap,
With a penchant for a nap.
The spoon dreams of flying high,
While dreaming stars pass by.

Whispers from the past arise,
Like pizza in disguise.
A clock that runs backward spins,
With laughter where pain begins.

Whimsical Narratives

Once a lemon wrote a tale,
Of a mouse who learned to sail.
In pajamas made of cheese,
They navigated the breeze.

A dancing fence, quite absurd,
Spoke to a passing bird.
Together, they found delight,
In a sky painted bright.

Lopsided Perspectives

A worm contemplating fate,
On the edge of a silver plate.
Sneakers untie, it seems quite fair,
As I trip over thin air.

Umbrellas wielding grand old plans,
Fight against the winds in bands.
Chickens dressed in polka dots,
Discuss the world with silver pots.

Smiles in the Peculiar

A cat wears shoes, what a sight,
Chasing shadows in the night.
A dog who dreams of taking flight,
In a world that feels just right.

Socks go missing by the pair,
The fridge has secrets, if you dare.
A parrot speaks in rhymes quite rare,
In this oddness, wonder's flair.

Bouncing frogs don jeweled crowns,
Silly hats in small-town towns.
Laughter hides in frowns and downs,
Where joy in silliness abounds.

So grab a snack, join the fun,
In this world where jest won't shun.
Life's a game that's never done,
In peculiar smiles, we all run.

Adventures in Anomaly

Bicycles with wings take flight,
As squirrels play chess in daylight.
A penguin in a business suit,
As fish sing songs from their pursuit.

Flamingos dance in bright pink tights,
While moonbeams wiggle in the nights.
A dragon dreams of purple heights,
In adventures full of sights.

Ghosts in pajamas sip their tea,
With polka-dots, so carefree.
A snail races with a bumblebee,
In this land of jubilee.

Join the strange, take off your hat,
Wear the joy, however flat.
In oddities, life's where it's at,
So tip your toes and chase a cat.

The Fine Line of Strange

A turtle wiggles in a dance,
With jellybeans, it takes a chance.
A toaster laughs at the romance,
Of breakfast dreams and their expanse.

Unicorns with polka-dot coats,
Swim through puddles, row tiny boats.
A hamster dreams of grander moats,
In life with funny antidotes.

Clouds turn into fluffy sheep,
As ice cream drips from dreams so deep.
A world where giggles never sleep,
In the oddest turns, we leap.

So twirl around and sing out loud,
In this strange life, be quite proud.
Embrace the weird, it's not a shroud,
For every laugh makes joy so loud.

Peculiar Portraits

A portrait of a cat in plaid,
With a grin that's slightly mad.
It wears a monocle so rad,
In colors bright, it looks so glad.

A fish catches sun in a hat,
While a lizard chats with a bat.
A quirky scene, imagine that,
Life's odd moments hold a spat.

Kites that giggle as they soar,
Flying high above the shore.
With laughter echoing galore,
In portraits painted, strange rapport.

So brush away your fears of plain,
In quirky art, there's joy to gain.
Embrace the silly, break the chain,
For in these tales, they'll dance in rain.

Avant-garde Adventures

In a world where squirrels can dance,
And bicycles wear funny hats,
Giraffes take selfies with their phones,
While cats spin records on their mats.

Frog chefs bake with sweet delight,
And turtles spin in disco lights,
The sun wears shades and sips cold tea,
What a party, wild and free!

Pigeons learning how to rhyme,
Waltzing frogs in perfect time,
Bubblegum clouds float in the sky,
As rainbows giggle passing by.

A walrus donning a top hat,
Dances with a dancing cat,
Life's a circus, all a jest,
In this wacky, quirky quest!

Riddles Wrapped in Time

Tick-tock clocks run backwards now,
As fish give speeches, take a bow,
While robots brew their morning tea,
And talk about philosophy.

Ladybugs play chess on leaves,
While caterpillars weave their dreams,
A turtle finds a hidden chest,
Full of socks; it's quite the quest!

Socks that dance and sing out loud,
Silly dreams that suit the crowd,
The world spins on its funny axis,
While elephants wear pink galas.

So if you think this all is mad,
Just join the fun, and you'll be glad,
For riddles wrap in every rhyme,
And laughter echoes through our time!

Euphoria in Eccentricity

A toaster sings while bread does toast,
As zebras paint and blue whales boast,
Monkeys cook in aprons bright,
Underneath the silver light.

Pineapples wear polka dots,
While cabbage plays the xylophone,
Dancing shoes on shoes of crocs,
Let the silliness be shown!

Sprinklers dance in the daytime sun,
While laughing clouds decide to run,
A parade of oddities we crave,
Within this world, all are brave!

And if you think it's all a joke,
Join the dance, don't be a yolk,
Embrace the madness, take a chance,
For life's a silly, joyful dance!

Curves in the Narrative

A teacup spins on roller skates,
While ducklings plan their dinner dates,
The moon juggles with the stars,
As coffee drips from candy jars.

Socks that match but don't quite go,
Spin around like they're on show,
And marmalade begins to skate,
Singing praises, feeling great.

Umbrellas sprout some funky wings,
As laughter's healing as it sings,
In this tale of ups and downs,
Where giggles wear the brightest crowns!

So if your heart feels light and free,
Join the wobbly jubilee,
For curves and quirks, oh, what a scene,
In life's grand play, where we can dream!

Portraits of the Absurd

In socks that fought and climbed the wall,
A cat who meows like a disco ball,
I stir my coffee with a shoe,
Wondering if that's what llamas do.

The toaster sings a tune so sweet,
While ants march 'round in tiny feet,
A broccoli tree stands proud and tall,
Demanding the peas come for a ball.

A fish in glasses reads the news,
While I debate on wearing shoes,
The moon winks at my morning toast,
Whispering secrets, it loves the most.

Dancing chairs in the living room,
Chasing dust bunnies with a broom,
Life's a circus in every nook,
You never know just where to look!

Revelations in Riddles

A pickle and an egg, they crossed the street,
Wearing tiny hats, oh, what a feat!
A dance-off with a cabbage head,
Twirling in rhythm, it's time for bed.

The clock's hands walked a mile today,
While the sun took a nap, and forgot to play,
Clouds dressed in pajamas, quite the sight,
Snoring softly in the fading light.

A jigsaw puzzle talks to an old shoe,
Explaining how gumbo can cure the flu,
I ponder if socks have dreams at night,
Of adventures that sparkle, oh what a fright!

The chair giggles, it tickles my sigh,
As I glance at the fridge, it's starting to cry,
Lost in the maze of my silly dreams,
Life is funnier than it always seems.

Surreal Musings on Routine

Every morning, my toast does a jig,
Winking at the butter, oh so big,
The clock melts down, a Dali sight,
Sipping coffee till it's midnight.

My cat wears glasses while reading the news,
Tattooed squirrels shout, "You've nothing to lose!"
The floor speaks secrets that tease my toes,
While the kitchen sings in pantomime prose.

A pineapple dons a tuxedoed style,
Whispering compliments, making me smile,
Meanwhile, my plants plot a mutiny,
Demanding tea while they sip at me.

With chaos dancing beneath a sun's glow,
Each day's a show with a twist we all know,
Life's odd little nuggets, shiny and bright,
Serve laughter as a savory bite.

Glimpses of the Extraordinary

A kangaroo hops through the local shop,
Buying ice cream, with an elegant flop,
It tries to juggle eggs and a hat,
While my goldfish plans a gossip spat.

A dancing broom sweeps out the blues,
And a mole in slippers refuses to snooze,
The clock tick-tocks in a jazzy beat,
Making daily chores feel much more sweet.

On Wednesdays, the walls try to sing,
Joining the furniture for an odd fling,
While the dog plays chess with a curious worm,
Building a world where all's an affirm.

Life's a gallery of strange little thoughts,
Throwing wild parties for those it forgot,
In each quirky moment, a wink or a grin,
You find the fabulous hiding within!

Enigmatic Whispers

In socks adorned with polka dots,
The cat debates a sock puppet's thoughts.
A toaster sings its morning tune,
While dancing spoons engage in a swoon.

A bird in shades struts down the lane,
Spilling laughter like summer rain.
The clock ticks backward, laughing loud,
As ants parade beneath a cloud.

A fish wears a hat, quite out of place,
Debating life's swift, winding race.
Bubblegum clouds float in the sky,
And reality giggles as moments fly.

With quirks aplenty and joy to share,
We ride the tide of this whimsical air.
Life's a circus, a delightful jest,
In this oddity, we find our rest.

Life's Absurd Jigsaw

Puzzles scattered, each piece askew,
A giraffe reads a poem to you.
Marshmallow trees in a candy land,
Salsa dancing, the squirrels all stand.

A snail races past in a slow-motion spree,
Wearing a top hat, it winks with glee.
Clouds with personalities float on by,
While rainbows trade jokes with the fireflies.

A frog plays chess, the stakes are high,
The queen is a butterfly, oh my!
Lollipops whisper tales of delight,
As upside-down stars twinkle at night.

Life's missing pieces fit with a laugh,
In this jumbled world, we find our path.
A gentle reminder, a twist of fate,
In absurdity's embrace, we celebrate.

Fractured Realities

A rainbow spills out across the street,
As penguins dressed in suits compete.
The sun wears a bowtie, gleaming bright,
While shadows gossip about the night.

A frog on a bicycle, wheels of cheese,
Pedals through fields of dancing trees.
A fox plays poker, chips made of straw,
While rabbits debate a lingering flaw.

Mirrors reflect what we seldom see,
Normalcy dancing like a bumblebee.
The grass giggles beneath the sky,
As time skips along, not shy to try.

With laughter and whimsy, the world's a jest,
In fractured moments, we find our rest.
Each oddity sparkles like stars at dawn,
In this surreal dance, we carry on.

Chasing Peculiar Dreams

A night owl plays chess with the moon,
While marshmallows float, a sweet balloon.
Turtles wearing sneakers jog along,
Singing a very peculiar song.

Balloons of laughter soar through the air,
As unicorns debate which star is rare.
A jellybean sun, so sugary bright,
Sends smiles rippling into the night.

In the pages of dreams, odd things conspire,
A fish teaching yoga on a tightrope wire.
Time does a dance, a silly tango,
While mismatched socks play a lonesome banjo.

Chasing after whimsies, we're never naive,
In this playful world, we dare to believe.
With wonder and laughter lighting the seams,
We wander through life, pursuing our dreams.

The Curious Canvas of Existence

In the morning, socks mismatch,
Tea spills on the living room mat.
Birds chirp secrets to the moon,
And cats plot world domination soon.

Pants made of polka dots sway,
As daydreams prance, then run away.
Neighbours argue with old tin cans,
While squirrels join in the dance of plans.

A dog wearing glasses chases flies,
While a goldfish skeptically sighs.
Laughter echoes down hallways,
As crumpled papers tell wild tales.

Yet in this chaos, a spark of cheer,
Glimmers through all the bizarre veneer.
With each odd twist, the heart must sing,
Embracing all that this life can bring.

Uncharted Realms of the Everyday

Umbrellas bloom in a sunny sky,
As bicycles waltz and pigeons fly.
A cat wears shoes to impress a dog,
While robots search for the finest fog.

Hot dogs dance at the city fair,
While clouds gossip without a care.
Chickens juggle on the front lawn,
And the toaster's been up since dawn.

A mirror shows reflections of dreams,
Where ice cream melts into puddle streams.
Origami birds plot their escape,
From the pantry's colorful landscape.

But through the maze of daily quirks,
Laughter hums as surprise lurks.
In odd corners where wonders hide,
Joy leaps out in the silliest ride.

Curiosities in Motion

An octopus dons a bowler hat,
While a frog gets tipsy, dancing flat.
Fish ride bikes on the sidewalk lane,
While robots sip tea, feeling quite sane.

Potato chips begin to chatter,
About their dreams and popcorn's platter.
Pens write stories of socks that roam,
As flying cows call their friends back home.

A snail lays claim to the tallest tree,
Claiming it's faster, oh can't you see?
Jellybeans tumble with joy and flair,
Creating candy rainbows in the air.

Yet through these whims and vibrant quests,
Laughter spins like a jester's jest.
In a world where oddities bloom,
We find delight in our splendid room.

Quirks of Existence

A pickle swims in lemonade seas,
As clouds wear hats and shake their knees.
Mice play chess in the old barn loft,
Debating over who is more soft.

Gumballs giggle, rolling down the street,
While cactus plants sway to a funky beat.
Umbrellas twirl in a sunny charm,
Where even the spoons learn to disarm.

Pancakes stack up, towering high,
Winking down with a buttery sigh.
Kites sail high on a windy spree,
Whispering secrets, just like me.

Amidst the absurd, joy takes flight,
Painting colors in the day and night.
In this playful world, let's dance and spin,
Finding laughter in where we've been.

Curious Echoes of Uncertainty

In a hat made of noodles, a frog sings loud,
It juggles odd marbles beneath a pink cloud.
A cat in a tuxedo plays chess by the sea,
While breezes blow kisses from a tall, swaying tree.

Bicycles whizzing, they're powered by cheese,
As turtles breakdance with incredible ease.
A donut-shaped planet spins round in delight,
With rainstorms of soda that douse all the fright.

Fish wear sunglasses, lounging on rocks,
And sheep write bestsellers, it really unlocks!
Through gardens of laughter, with flowers that giggle,
We dance through the nonsense and let our hearts wiggle.

Oh, the squirrels hold debates on who steals more nuts,
While the moon winks and grins, showing off funny cuts.
So let's raise our glasses, to all that is strange,
For life's funniest moments are often deranged.

Whispers from the Edge of Normalcy

A penguin in slippers strolls down the lane,
While a pig plays the trumpet, not shy of the rain.
They tap dance with crickets beneath the streetlight,
As shadows jump ropes in the pale moonlight.

Samurai squirrels are locking up stores,
With candy-coated hammers and bubblegum roars.
And llamas in sunglasses giggle with glee,
Playing poker with lions near the old oak tree.

A toaster sings opera, while bread does its thing,
And elephants juggle with grace on the swing.
To the beat of a drum made of jelly and cheese,
Life's odd little antics bring smiles with ease.

Let's cherish the madness that dances on air,
For in every odd corner, there's laughter to share.
As whimsy unfurls all around with a grin,
The edge of the usual is where jokes begin.

Jigsaw Pieces of the Unusual

A pencil fights paper in a never-made war,
As a turtle paints portraits of candy and more.
Forks start a band where they strum on fine plates,
And we chuckle at pirate mice planning their fates.

The clouds turn to popcorn, the sky smells like fun,
And the sun wears a crown made of toasted cinnamon.
While beetles in tuxedos debate the best snack,
As the days fade to colors we can't hold back.

A spoon and a knife bask in golden sunset,
Swapping tall tales, though they never forget.
While rabbits in top hats do card tricks in parks,
Making wishes with candles lit up by their sparks.

Let's dance with the bizarre, no map needed here,
For in every odd twist, we find reasons to cheer.
Life's puzzle just might be a quirky delight,
As laughter shapes shadows that dance through the night.

Dancing Shadows on a Shifting Path

A chicken on stilts marches down the street,
While jellybeans waltz on their sticky, sweet feet.
With goggles on frogs and marshmallows afloat,
The world plays a melody we all love to quote.

A cactus in ballet shoes twirls with a flair,
As daisies all giggle, spreading joy everywhere.
With cupcakes as dancers, the stage is alive,
And the rhythm of whimsy makes everyone thrive.

A monkey in pajamas swings high in the trees,
Trading secrets with parrots that speak with a breeze.
Oh, the world is a circus where fun is the king,
While dreams ride on bicycles, joy taking wing.

We'll prance down the path where the shadows grow long,
With laughter as fuel, forever our song.
In a world bursting forth from the oddly profound,
Each moment of magic is where we are found.

Unraveled Threads

A sock escapes, it does its dance,
Twirling and swirling like it's in a chance.
The cat looks on with curious glee,
Wondering who the true wild one could be.

Adventures unfold in the laundry room,
While T-shirts dream of escaping their gloom.
The dryer hums a lullaby song,
While mismatched haikus stretch all night long.

A pair of shoes, one left, one right,
Ignored for ages, take flight in the night.
With tiny wings made of lint and dust,
They venture forth in a mission of trust.

So let the threads unravel, go roam,
For in oddities, we might find a home.
Next time you're folding, don't take it to heart,
For silliness binds us, a strange work of art.

Shadows of the Unforeseen

A shadow creeps upon the wall,
It resembles a creature, oh what a thrall!
It wiggles and giggles, plays peek-a-boo,
Leaving us wondering what next it will do.

Chairs turn into palaces in the dark,
While the broomstick whispers, 'Let's take a lark!'
The clock strikes twelve, mice wear a crown,
As unleashed dreams come tumbling down.

There's a strange brew boiling in the pot,
With chicken and socks, it's piping hot!
And who's stirring? A rat with flair,
Twirling spoons while pulling at air.

So watch your shadows as they prance,
In corners of laughter, we leap and dance.
For unforeseen wonders abound in the day,
When ordinary feels just a tad too cliche.

Exaggerated Realities

A banana slips with a grand ballet,
Bananas in tuxedos, oh what a display!
The kitchen erupts in a fruit-filled fight,
As oranges gather for a citrus delight.

A book falls open, tales jump from the page,
As characters argue, fueled by their rage.
An octopus dresses in lovely pink lace,
While the cat struts by, holding its face.

The toaster's possessed, it's humming a tune,
While waffles plot how to steal the moon.
And pancakes declare it's their rightful due,
To reign supreme in this breakfast zoo.

So join the circus of everyday grace,
Where battles are fought in a cheerful space.
Embrace the absurdity tucked in your way,
For realities can dance and sway in the fray.

Whims of Fate

A turtle rides on a skateboard, what fun,
Zooming past bees who bask in the sun.
It spins and it twirls, a show on the street,
While onlookers chuckle, can't stay in their seat.

And fish wear top hats, quite dapper and spry,
Holding a meeting on how to fly high.
They debate over currents with foam in a glass,
Planning a route where the seagulls won't pass.

A cabbage rolls by with a spunky little strut,
Dreaming of being a famous donut.
While tomatoes laugh in their vibrant red coats,
As dreams intertwine, finding all of their notes.

So ride the rollercoaster of silly fate,
Where the strange and absurd intertwine while we wait.
In the carnival of life, take a chance,
For whimsy is fleeting — come join in the dance!

Whims in the Wind

A cat walks by with a bow tie on,
While squirrels debate which way to run.
A park bench dances, or so I think,
Sprinklers rhyme in a puddle's blink.

Clouds wear hats, it's quite a sight,
As grass starts giggling under the light.
Cupcakes float by, don't ask me why,
I'll take one home; oh my, oh my!

The sun decides to wear stripes today,
While shadows start to prance and sway.
Birds play chess, but lose to the breeze,
And I just sit here, laughing with ease.

In this world where oddities play,
Each moment is a show in its way.
So grab your umbrella and dancing shoes,
Let's tango with whimsy, and never lose!

Mysteries in Mundanity

A pen rolls off and makes a dash,
While spoons conspire to stage a clash.
The toaster giggles when bread's not near,
Is that a laugh, or just my cheer?

The clock ticks slow, then speeds away,
As socks revolt, refusing to stay.
Dust bunnies form a band on the floor,
With each little hop, they want to explore.

A rubber duck swims in my cup,
Squeaks a tune as I try to sup.
Pillows conspire in a fluffy maze,
And I'm just lost in this blanket daze.

Every moment's a riddle, it seems,
Unraveling laughter through the mundane dreams.
Join the symphony of this merry grind,
For joy is found in the quirks we find!

The Astonishing Normal

A squirrel wears glasses and reads the news,
While sidewalks morph into slippery crews.
Chickens in hats learn to do the cha-cha,
While pigeons are painting their next panorama.

Tea kettles whistle a comedic tune,
As lampshades plot to dance by the moon.
Have you seen the dog with a mustache?
Oh, what a sight—it's quite a bash!

Jellybeans tumble from trees above,
Inviting the bees to a party of love.
The fridge hums softly, a lullaby sweet,
As everyone joins for this quirky feat.

In a world where the normal's askew,
Every glance sparks a giggle anew.
So let's raise a toast to curious things,
For in this oddity, wild joy springs!

Tangled Realms of Reality

A worm in a tie gives speeches all day,
While ants are organizing a grand ballet.
A shoe with a wink cascades down the street,
And I can't help but tap my feet.

Mirrors stare back with something to say,
As shadows stretch, then giggle away.
Cacti are gossiping, tall and proud,
While clouds make faces in a wandering crowd.

A fish wore a crown and swam in a bowl,
Claiming his title of 'Ruler of Soul.'
Meanwhile, the carpet began to tell tales,
Of knights and dragons, and talking snails.

Each twist and turn in this wondrous ride,
Turns dull ordinary into vibrant tide.
So come along, and let's jump in line,
In this tangled dance, where laughter shines!

Playful Oddities

In socks that rarely match their kin,
A dance of color does begin.
Chickens cluck in synchronized time,
While cats compose in perfect rhyme.

The teapot sings a twisty tune,
As spoons and forks start to commune.
A frog in hats and velvet shoes,
Declares that all the world's good news.

Noses twitch as squirrels wear ties,
Arguing if it's wrong or wise.
The moon is made of cheddar cheese,
While bees are buzzing "Take it, please!"

So raise a cup to life's delight,
Embrace the odd, from morn till night.
For laughter is a vibrant spice,
In our odd world that's full of nice.

Chronicles of the Uncommon

A turtle with a marketing plan,
Sells ice cream from a frying pan.
Giraffes in bow ties roam the street,
While penguins serve us lemonade neat.

The toaster thinks it's on a spree,
Popping toast like confetti.
Dinosaurs play hopscotch on clouds,
As jellybeans cheer in colorful crowds.

A fish in glasses gives a speech,
On topics that are far from reach.
Kangaroos compete in a race,
With pockets full of dreams to chase.

So join the dance, the quirky parade,
In every corner, oddities invade.
A tale as tall as the tallest tree,
In whimsical worlds, we long to be.

Fleeting Shadows of Silliness

A cloud dressed up as a fancy hat,
On top of a dog that's chasing a cat.
A fish that juggles with three bright bowls,
While ants debate the meaning of roles.

Balloons take flight in a crazy race,
While cupcakes sport their very own lace.
Wandering gnomes with peculiar hats,
Join a tango of playful spats.

The clock chimes then skips a bit,
Saying "Catch me if you can; don't sit!"
A rocking chair sings the blues at night,
As rabbits bounce towards the moonlight.

With every chuckle, let laughter ring,
In shadows where silly puppets spring.
These fleeting moments, a gift so sweet,
Are oddities life serves us to greet.

Hues of Peculiarity

A rainbow dips in a steaming stew,
As mice in tuxedos bid adieu.
A cactus dreams of becoming a tree,
In a world that sways so free.

Socks parade, with flair they show,
In patterns only they can know.
The sun wears glasses, soaking rays,
While squirrels delight in quirky plays.

A snail in roller skates does glide,
While a broomstick takes a wild ride.
Frogs gossip 'neath the silver moon,
While ducks recite a funny tune.

So splash in colors, bright and bold,
In every corner, life's stories unfold.
With hues of laughter, let joy inspire,
And dance with oddities that never tire.

www.ingramcontent.com/pod-product-compliance
Lightning Source LLC
Chambersburg PA
CBHW051641160426
43209CB00004B/741